searching for eastman

searching for eastman

a performance poem

charles c smith

MAWENZI
HOUSE

We acknowledge the support of the Canada Council for the Arts for our publishing program. We also acknowledge support from the Government of Ontario through the Ontario Arts Council, and the support of the Government of Canada through the Canada Book Fund.

Cover design by Sabrina Pignataro

Cover photos: Punnarong / Abstract hand playing piano keyboard watercolor illustration painting background. stock photo / istockphoto.com; pyzhova / Abstract scanned digital pixel noise glitch background stock photo / istockphoto.com

Library and Archives Canada Cataloguing in Publication

Title: Searching for Eastman : a performance poem / Charles C. Smith.

Names: Smith, Charles C., 1953- author.

Identifiers: Canadiana (print) 20210302372 | Canadiana (ebook) 20210302658 | ISBN 9781774150535 (softcover) | ISBN 9781774150542 (EPUB) | ISBN 9781774150559 (PDF)

Classification: LCC PS8637.M5595 S43 2021 | DDC C811/.6—dc23

Printed and bound in Canada by Coach House Printing

Mawenzi House Publishers Ltd.
39 Woburn Avenue (B)
Toronto, Ontario M5M 1K5
Canada
www.mawenzihouse.com

searching for eastman

for julius eastman (1940-90)

a reminder to those who think they can destroy liberators by acts of treachery, malice, and murder . . . [l]ike all organizations, especially governments and religious organizations, they oppress in order to perpetuate themselves. their methods of oppression are legion. but when they find that their more subtle methods are failing, they resort to murder. even now, in my own country, my own people, my own time, gross oppression and murder still continue. julius eastman

text by charles c smith in collaboration with the performers

CONTENTS

INTRODUCTION

searching for eastman is a multidisciplinary performance in 4 acts based on the interpretation of four of eastman's compositions through poetry, theatre, music, dance, and video. these pieces are: (1) evil nigger; (2) prelude to st joan; (3) stay on it; and (4) gay guerrilla. this work is a choreopoem whose roots trace through the african griot tradition, the harlem renaissance (eg the work of langston hughes with katherine dunham and kurt weill), the black arts movement (eg amiri baraka's work with sun ra) and defined as "a form of dramatic expression that combines poetry, dance, music, and song . . . (as) first coined in 1975 by ntozake shange in a description of her work, *for colored girls who have considered suicide / when the rainbow is enuf.*

each act reveals something of eastman's life, from childhood on with particular attention to his being caught between worlds, neither home in black or queer spaces during times of turbulence related to these identities. the first act checks in on how such a persona came to be, the construction of this liminal space in the myopic stasis of 1950s mccarthyism sanitized suburban america followed by the hot political 1960s' focus on freedom and identities. the second act unfolds his core practice, its methods and madness, the controversies he was at the heart of in the emerging canon of american minimalism, his seeming yearning for martyrdom. the third act is that of his relationships, torrid and engaging, short and destructive, demanding. the final act is his rebellion as warrior guerrilla, abandoned and alone, disappearing into the nebulous world of homelessness, drugs and alcohol.

each act is structured in time with eastman's music to honour his work and the stories he seemed to be telling in them. also, there are moments in between each piece where the audience will be able to participate by reading his words, or words of others about him, while associated images appear on screen.

searching for eastman engages scenarios through the spirit of memories, sketched in poetry and drawn out through movement/dance, digital imaging and music. as an immersive experiential approach, there is little direct dialogue, and each section forms something of a contribution to a collective eulogy, one built on astonishment at his untimely death along with memories of his greatness and his equally great self-destructiveness that was finally his undoing.

the voices here are composite based on the contributors to the recently released book *gay guerrilla: julius eastman and his music*. the words look to capture the spirit of their experiences of eastman.

since eastman in his lifetime was more amongst white people, they speak to him more in memory, and regret. the black voices speak to his discovery, now, and to those who came before him. they speak to him as an innovator seeing the arts through the barrier-bending ways he portrayed his identities, the intersections between his racialized/politicized/sexualized selves.

the basic stage design is tompkins park as it was in the 1980s—a hangout for heroin addicts and those looking for hook-ups.

the "place" in which the action happens is in a world beyond the physical. the black cast embody the spirits of eastman's ancestors and bring out to him the connection to a suppressed but known past; the contradictions of eastman's own time; and now, where black queer identity is firmly embedded in the leadership of black radical activism, ie, black lives matter and solidarity with indigenous peoples and others historically marginalized, ie, those who self-identify as mad and its links with the impact of colonization and anti-black racism.

the storyteller is the griot who is witness to the recitations and interactions between the characters and the characters interactions with the video and digital.

the "non-blacks" are the voices of those who knew eastman and are now recounting his talents and outlandish life choices. "the next generation" are young artists drawn to eastman and his work and discovering their own identities, privileged and otherwise, in the context of becoming aware and moving to understand and enact solidarity.

in the spaces between pieces, those present will be invited to read words of and about eastman. this will happen as paper text is lowered to certain parts of the audience and the lights shone there. those sitting in this space will be asked to stand, or sit, pull down and read aloud the text. when the words are pulled down, a corresponding image should appear on screen as if in dialogue with the reader.

CHARACTERS AND SETTING

african ancestor

black spirit

black being then

black being now

storyteller/griot

white researcher

non-black from another continent

white person

2 next generation appear in *gay guerrilla*—they can be of any identity

ACT I

evil nigger

scene: tompkins park in the 1980s, otherwise known as "needle park". this space on the lower east side, alphabet city, in manhatten is home to drug addicts, runaways, those recently released from prison. its benches and tables are splintered and, in some instances, broken. trash, bottles of cheap whiskey, wine and empty beer cans strewn about

eastman voice-over repeated as the characters walk in silent circles: "what i mean by is, that thing which is fundamental; that person or thing that attains to a basicness of a fundamentalness, and eschews that which is superficial, or, could we say, elegant . . . there are 99 names of allah, and there are 52 niggers"

the last three minutes we hear eastman's voice while the music winds down. this leads into "prelude to st joan"

scene i

STORYTELLER/GRIOT

with what there is to know   and all that fits like stones
within memory   once known then forgotten as if a dream

not wanting to be told   censured in grieving

remembered now as flames   reborn and roaming
the borders of new york   ithaca buffalo vienna

ballet classes piano stools   concert halls decked in black
the gay underground   village of subway washrooms

10 a.m. whiskey in a trench coat   rehearsals
in black leather and chains   on the lower east side—

his buffalo house   a white space   open to many
he dropped things there   clothes and lovers

the homeless man he invited in   who took him for a ride

those unpredictable notes   in his improvised compositions
evil nigger stay on it prelude to st joan gay guerrilla—

that deep baritone   mad as a king   a supplicant saint
defiant in a sinister all-consuming rage   fingers ploughing
pianos

and cellos groaning the weight   of spirit memories—

an anomaly   the music stuck to his skin
would not let him be   and carried him into oblivion

away from singleterry   and the brooklyn philharmonia
who matched his notes   with some sense of belonging

quivering in a form that would not offer itself   nor set aside
provenance in a common hue   and what that fueled him
to do

once the forbidden tomes of sex and skin   let him loose like
a knife

sharpened on the edge of disdain   his complete
and utter deliverance   into what he did   and how—

and with whom?   and the terms he set for sharing? with
only a few following?   out of love? sex? disbelief?

angling like small children   held close then left astray—

but was he ever open enough   to let anything else in?
such lightning in stories   his music and imagination

his strange and sudden   arrivals departures
at the loading gate   of the ephemeral

the branding of a label   he would live to regret—

so instead of a sinecure   did he seek out the "sin to cure"?
with little regard for anything   especially himself

and those years he went missing   with none aware of his
passing
until eight months after   a small capture of words in
the "village voice"

reminding those who abandoned him   of his time and telling
that blistering hypnotic succulence   his acapella
tongues and notes

dance and 10 cellos 8 hands   on four grand pianos—

it is this telling   his dark hangouts and hoods
his tumbling turning falling alone   a wanderer wounded

cloistered into timelessness   a sodden mystery like no other
with so many before without sequence   and several
  coming after

he found the branch   it cracked through his telling
and he fell   black icarus without angel wings in america

scene ii

ANCESTOR

he was our child   water spirit
bathed in brine and oil   sharing sweat

the beauty of our shadows   and their glow
in those secluded spaces   we know—

they say there were none   before him
what would they know   i come to speak our names

mati   malungo   malongue batiment   sippi mahu
tongzhi   igbo women staying british guns with spears

azandi quimbanda mzili   kitesha tinkonkana eshenga
mwanga and his baptized celibates   chanting death

they couldn't   wouldn't see
our arms asleep in vespers   our members

pouring into openings   sublime and wet
tongues   without words washing

inside nights' belly on the hunt   beneath starlit
leaves   and the baobab's boughs   bent into wisdom—

on soft cloth our legs   our lips and fingers scathing
the echoing silence   of pleasure and tenderness

he gave all of himself   as we did
then found ourselves alone   without comfort

on a journey across endless waters
coiled in chains   shanties and long fields

hiding our shadows   with our shame
our loins purloined   for production

under a wooden cross   bearing a dead man
broken   and burying everything below him that did not kneel

BLACK BEING THEN

it is thunder   how i want this clap in my ear
shango's tree-trunk   sexy black thighs

scaling mau mau mountains   earth-pounding
step-by-step   across a martyred "jungle" space

such "evil" shrouded in blackness   his balls
dancing above lips

he used the word "nigger" this way   to describe
the past as future   its wax holding everything

in place   this world away he came from
disguised   bared in boats' bellies' darkness

our bodies   bearded into each other soft bone
foam and waves   an overwhelming deep

that cross of hunger   dangling atop stairs

a mirror on stone buildings   he entered
loathing such heightened   palaces of fear—

known as a child   stubborn and showing
his father moved on   this glimpse in his wandering eyes

he escaped into what he could not help but boldly blindly be

and speaks now   from attica's darkest cell
dripping sweat and semen   spit and blood

the thugs and bullets   black sticks and gun fire

to stonewall's deepest caves   passers-by
flashing towels in sweated saunas   seeking sex

to outing cage on stage in buffalo
charring that master's red face—

he did what he did and never once explained
only the moment mattered its randomness bawdy and mad

and for this he was left everywhere ahead yet behind
the white walls in front his every breath and scream—

it was his will to contend undefined definitive defamed
defrocked and rocked into echoes of public washrooms

his scripts buried in trash his ensembles bleeding like fleas
every nerve so purposefully lewd loud-mouthed and open

a thirst between needles scotch whisky
outside ivied university walls feint with praise

until long after his body returned some time ago
like water to the earth . . .

BLACK BEING NOW

i found his words
as if they were mine

this was not "el cimarron"
that rebel with respect and decency

caught between the teeth of steel demons
held on screen in the master's stroke—

he did not want a veil as ceiling wall as bar
his body silenced like a thief

with blood pumping purple sparks
his heart in vast occult shade

arteries wide open
a trap he set for others caught him

breathing his own way
rumbling through torment and fear

the agonies plagued upon his bed
sheets bath houses subway washrooms

a long way from ithaca buffalo rotting inside the apple

suckling a bottle somewhere in his coat pocket
markings notable up his sleeves

attica stonewall black bodies beneath police guns
and men unearthed in a toronto garden

his eyes mirroring windows
each day the blues of the rostrum

a train stops at his station the whistle blares
steam rises from the side of the tracks

this journey always beginning
never done

scene iii

CHORUS OF NON-BLACK VOICES
a 5'8" lean   bass baritone even in whispers sings possessed
dedicated depraved   lost in vapors of a hungering self

never at ease   turning on everyone he knew
then himself   a blister of brilliant blindness mired and
  estranged

we see him on stage   beside four pianos a string quartet
ten cellos a film score   artaud grimacing in an early role

bleeding robeson   in a western gait
an uneasy stretch   piano voice and composition

fingers pounding keys   the fire of burundi drums
heard so disturbing   the litmus of his alchemy and certainty

and a memory of his father   lost to sharing
who before had cared for many   a child parent

took his days   his every second dripping
neglect   and absolute abstinence

RESEARCHER
but was this memory swallowing him?   like rapids
crashing rocks   when he walked down narrow winter streets?
those cold sterile places   tompkins park
addicts and potholes   wood rotting
public benches   thick white snow

holding all things real and imaginary
like street signs full of warning
hanging in pale grey skies

ANOTHER CONTINENT

and each step before him   was a tributary
full of laughter and crowded
with sleepless adolescent boys
masturbating in a subway washroom

with stray men in a stool next to his lover
his orgasm rising from a thin plastic syringe
bleeding hallucinogens

WHITE PERSON

this told him something sacred   with words
spiraling skyward from a bowl in an open field
frankincense sliding through a halo of thorns
in blue winter air

one voice reads first couplet. all join for the 2nd and 3rd couplet and line. one voice reads final couplet

and with each breeze he continued   his face
caught in the shadows of green gems   ears

loaded into sockets full of pain   cheeks
collapsing into canyons deep as death   and his

forehead brushed like a whisper   formed in the night

eyes weeping as if in a graveyard   at the outskirts
of dark and noisy tents   of a tropical bazaar

in chorus to start. after 2nd couplet, one stops reading and joins the dance. another leaves after the next 2 couplets and the final reader joins the dance at the end

a 5'8" lean   bass baritone even in whispers sings possessed
dedicated depraved   lost in vapors of a hungering self

loaded into sockets full of pain   cheeks
collapsing into canyons deep as death

we see him on stage   beside four pianos a string quartet
ten cellos a film score   artaud grimacing in an early role

fingers pounding keys   the fire of burundi drums
caught in the shadows of sapphire and bronze

his forehead brushed like a whisper   formed in the night

eyes weeping as if in a graveyard   at the outskirts
of the dark and noisy tents   of a tropical bazaar

scene iv

the griot returns with selected sections from the introductory poem

ACT 2

st joan

scene: a one-room apartment that is nearly empty

st joan is done with the three choruses speaking at the same time. they are on stage, moving before the music and then speaking as the music starts—robed/hooded, with video images of eastman from his performance 8 songs for a mad king. *the voices continue as the the african spirit, black beings and ancestor/eastman movements grasp the look and contrast of eastman's words, images related to the invocation of the saints he names*

each chorus repeats their parts simultaneously twice before moving on to the full chorus and, after that, moving on to the next set of words. in other words, they would each read their first part, move into chorus, then the second part followed by chorus. this is to be repeated throughout and often they play mixing up the words

the voice(s) reflect eastman's deep spirituality and how that coursed through his body, in all ways—music, alcohol, dance, sex, obscenities and madness. the voices conflate eastman's vast and sharp range of thoughts/emotions and his approach to composition, performance, being, his (and others) mumbling and self-doubt, affirmation, capturing how captivating, desperate and dangerous he was

the movement/dance by the african spirit, black beings and griot, begin just before the music starts

scene i

WHITE PERSON CHORUS

"lines with black note heads"   tempo mm144
each half staff ending   in any octave
high or low   cleverly ambiguous save for virtuousity

melodic frameworks   recurring fragmented descending
"f-e-d" with "d" "d" "d"   a half note
and "continuo figure"   a bass pattern at 1:30

semi-optional   whenever it appears and appears
at 13:25 1:80 12:30   a half-note for four or two black note heads

opening motive "evil nigger"   treads in the dark cells
this way with its limits   so many in the hills of folly
with a red satin cape   a mystic priest caught in the
  shallowness of despair

(what is a black man doing here?   an open queer?
in this indecipherable blindness   full of ego and greed?)

ANOTHER CONTINENT CHORUS

d minor scales into d-e-f-g-a-b'
cf in with 1:30 2:40 without new pitches
5:40 circle of 5ths of 5ths of 5ths

no more no more no more
where it was all taking talking walking
evil black and queer   stonewall and attica

colleagues in the same bow tie and jeans
in different (at times) sex and skin
and to pretend this was an escape

but what was missing in this thin space
catapulted into voice without sound or season
slipping into irreverence as revulsion

(let him be what he wants   drag queen and s&m?
in his own space his own time   but not at my front door)

RESEARCHER CHORUS

and in that descending evening of madness, he stood alone,
  at the precipice
wind whipping him, a torrent of suffering, wild and unyielding

black scarf fluttering, black-peaked cap, black lapel an essence
of his deliberate ease, his mostly pyrrhic moments when

his heart and veins, their shallow perforated vessels, their
disturbing speed, plunged downward into a drain out of hell

and its lesser places, the obscure challenging
passages of silence, prayer and grace, he came to

reveal, the studious pistons of his birth
as they hammered him, again and again, out of ignorance

into the wet august wind, boomerang blistering heat

(black and queer   a black queer a queer black
in a time when it seemed   nobody wanted him)

FULL CHORUS

cf and om at 6:30   om to d minor continuing at 7:15
8:30 marks the sequence   d-flat an original key (?)
the om and d minor only   again and again

d minor scales into d-e-f-g-a-b'
cf in with 1:30 2:40 without new pitches
5:40 circle of 5ths of 5ths of 5ths

scene ii

RESEARCHER CHORUS

i met him, then, a forager in a courtyard, a lonely visionary
clinging like a blaze, to a piece of bent copper

turned lime green, on a skyscraper's ledge, and he
looked at this as if he were a ghost, alone in a closet

carrying memories of brothers, sisters, friends
like detached heads, in a picnic basket

full of dried white and red roses, in full bloom—

yet he still got the clock on the church its view
above the brick red and black iron schoolhouse

its face dotted with windows telling him every second
this is the way the world is surrounded by time—

green grass turning blades brown hides
under snow comes again spring summer and fall

mallards and geese green wings imprint
ceramic clouds against the gun-metal smoke

of skyscrapers out of passing sunrise eventual sunset
from one portal of time into another—

ANOTHER CONTINENT CHORUS

this is no ordinary magic it's a ruse
and the still perfect silence of another life

he walked beside without a word
into the deliberate open space of day

where he saw paradigms of light stretched
into the merciless chaos of a sky

spray painted a purple chemical haze
where he wondered alone into the cold breathe of winter

pushing through horizons of twilight

and mourning that left his heart ached
in a world so astoundingly puerile there was

no moment when the white clock face
chimed out its powerlessness and fear

(did he tell time? how so when his music didn't? when
the lines he walked were chalk powdering his own
wintered face?)

WHITE PERSON CHORUS
or looking out of windows shaped by horror
cool bells ringing on hillsides echoes of fear
where the earth revolves like a brushstroke
thru the black and starlit galaxy
a painting by an idiot savant
blessed with a horoscope of the damned

youthful wings beat in this blue air
and he arrived at this cold hotel bar
with a hypnotic fantasy full
of nightly fears and steady
admonitions of the cold
unmarked journey of the bereaved

gale force winds howled like murder
in these borders and the surf beat
against dry shells of abandoned crabs
when he moved slowly thru the room
as if it were a forest curled in mists with reptiles
sharing secrets in the endless pounding rains

(and all of this wrapped itself in the glitter of the dead
a gift for him an ethos sketched with pathways to the deceased)

scene iii

CHORUS
prominent melodic recurrence   every 90 seconds
shifts   descending f-e-d   and then dddddddddd
in half notes   and then the "continuo figure" at 1:30

cf and om at 6:30   om to d minor continuing at 7:15
8:30 marks the sequence   d-flat an original key (?)
the om and d minor only   again and again

d minor scales into d-e-f-g-a-b'
cf in with 1:30 2:40 without new pitches
5:40 circle of 5ths of 5ths of 5ths

This was the Martin Luther King era, and I remember one time especially when Julius made me very proud. Kathleen Crofton, I learned some years later, didn't take me in her company originally because of my color. Eventually she did, though I was the only black person in the company. Crofton employed an Asian pianist for classes and rehearsals who used to play from scores. At the time, we were rehearsing Les Biches *with a famous British guest ballerina who had been brought in to choreograph the piece. The staff accompanist got sick at the last minute and couldn't be there to play the Poulenc score, so I suggested that Crofton engage Julius as a substitute. Julius came to the studio having never seen the big ballet score before. He looked it over a couple of times and began playing. He was even able to conduct the rehearsal with the dancers. Everybody was so amazed that this guy (and the only other black person there besides me) was able to look at this huge score and tune in right away. People were just wowed, and I was so proud.*

Weeks later, at the end of February, Eastman appeared as "guest artist" in a modern ballet based on Jean Genet's The Blacks, *which was produced by UB dance professor Cristyne Lawson and her Company of Man. Choreographed and directed by Lawson,* Black Ivory *was "a ballet for masked spectators and players." The title alludes to a trade name of the nineteenth century describing the human cargoes dispatched as merchandise from Africa to the markets of the "civilized" world. The score was by Roberto Laneri. Upon arrival at the Albright-Knox Art Gallery Sculpture Court where the event took place, audience members were asked to choose between two entrances to the performance area. At each entrance, audience members were issued a standard mask, which they were requested to put on. Only once they are inside the court do the audience members realize they have been segregated into an area for white-masked people and, on the other side of the court, people with black masks. The space between them is the stage for the action of* Black Ivory. *(28)*

ACT 3

stay on it

scene: a gay bar on the lower east side in new york

00 – 1:15 dancers only. eastman in a bar and in his own thoughts. he is approached by others who want to flirt with him. movements are sexy, seductive, swaggering

scene i

1:15 GRIOT
glitter glitter glitter cheeks and brow
sparkling lashes finger and toe nails
long curly blonde wigs swaying naked necks
rainbow mascara rouge lips and bright teeth
above that tight blue banana-shaped sarong

slit thighs lace sequins feathers and plumes
hot flashing flesh atop stilettos on a runway
a swinging double long necklace of pearls
red gloves sapphire nylons silk thongs and bras
with cigarettes laughing into a mirror of dreams

outside shut doors dim hallways and bedrooms
with oils makeup candles and cheeks
sweet baby legs and red leather jeans
boots and chains mouths and hands

alongside rustin taylor langston baldwin
cross-dressed sylvester jackie kaufman
on black genet magic "querrelle"
insatiable foils doubling sexual
in fassbinder's hungover fascist state

each step each moment submerged
dissing "decadence" giving and taking
atop egyptian cotton indian silk
or in rush hour subway washrooms

what sang in that queer black body was shrill
semen staining like a martyr's spit
churned from an insistence of pain
waged like torches lit beneath all needs

and wandering spirit worlds without a passport
or any verifiable source of self

except a voice that was never a whisper
suddenly one day long after now heard

scene ii

3:10 ANCESTOR
he knew he was treacherous blistering uncertain
his breath contesting guilt in this quagmire of greed

of those who claimed our tongues our clothes our sex

and named our boys in women's wear
whom deng prophets' spirit guides in ritual ordained

who witnessed nzinga the woman king and her male wives
wearing scarves ornaments and dresses waist to heel

and the ganga-ya-chibanda cross-dressed grandmother
   shamans
and the sipolio with surutya earrings and long gowns
   sweeping the earth

who saw the hutsi tutsi mirundi priests in sun-lit garments
   and masks
and mudoko dako awes florid clothes and hair

who stumbled upon new year festivals' mwaka oga or men
   in mbenda
swinging veils and burkina faso sorones' promising their
   first born male

and mashoga drags at weddings playing pembe
dancing and singing on chagkacha's pleasure trails

who logged the ngambo mumemke hanithi cross-dressers
their boys in public strip tease in headdress and lace

and zande warriors gifting spears as dowry with feasts
and nuban londos mesakin tubele parting goats and wares—

these were who we were and come from so now go to
as we do seeing our blood usurped and our bodies

pressed into darkness by murderous fools

4:55 BLACK CHORUS
garments veiling love-lust in candles and mist
thighs toes assess nipples tongues and lips

we dreamed our dress and desire without question
the omani khanith yan dauda in full veils

ANCESTOR
the lagedris in dahomy their chosen youth advising kings
and fon boys taking gaglgo "women"

BLACK BEING THEN
nzema bridals in ghana paved by dowry

the bala bitesha neither female nor male
and senagelese gor-digen in dresses make-up and braided hair

BLACK BEING NOW
somehow what others found troubled their sex

and we were astonished with what they wrote
our ways without our words wearied with meaning

purged by pagan parcels of storm and fire
cities and altars we knew but did not seek—

we then walked our days after their arrival
only in death escape or sleep

parsing memory's quill of what was once our skies

ANCESTOR AND BLACK BEING THEN
where the bruised wheel of joy and sorrow swam in breezes
planting pleasure and pain in the bends of flesh

ANCESTOR AND BLACK BEING NOW
where those before us rose out of the earth behind the faces
of trees
and the lines of brown-green horizons burst piñatas of cloud

not defined by any one thing or source of any difference
held suspect by the blasts of some misguided creed

BLACK BEING THEN AND BLACK BEING NOW
crafted inside distant halls
spaces soldiers shrouded in stone and savagery

keeping on to whomever fell within range
and guiding superiors surplices surveyors

through villages and outstretched lands
they fell upon clinging like weeds

ALL (SPIRIT AND BLACK BEING NOW LEAVE AFTER FIRST TWO LINES)
in episodes they called freedom
ripping blood and bones from breath and birth

BLACK BEING THEN AND ANCESTOR (BLACK BEING LEAVES AFTER THESE TWO LINES)
forcing merciless journeys
far from the savannahs and our visions of a place

ANCESTOR
we knew they would be loathe to enter

scene iii

7:15 NON-BLACK CHORUS
glitter glitter glitter straps and lace
ebony boots knee-high sparkles tasting thirsty thighs

sweet sky sweating sermons
dancing on sun-glanced avenues

the glow of balance before extinction
what plays serpent in the harmony of ears

what was then before we set it otherwise
spaces we called primitive to fill our needs

paved road railways shipyards guns and wear

ANOTHER CONTINENT
they did not fit what we had shaped
language garments color sex

their simple rude and unusual gaze
praising home-made altars carrying remnants of their dead

WHITE PERSON
and men who were women in sandals
long dresses hair raised in waves or braids

we found them in such cover so readily seen
then turned on our morals like a sword of guilt

this held us aloft from such insipid incest
a detour from our own adventures

RESEARCHER
we only saw what was and held ourselves
blasting boulders barreling down hills

we named this strange behavior with our pens
to set the dreams of those back home

who longed for stories
from the lands of bastard black beasts

CHORUS
and this is what we wanted to see
intoxicated in exotic fantasies

schooled by peculiar moments inside rooms
curtained in varied malevolent fabrics of fear

our didactic spaces of ruthlessness
thorns of belligerence perfume and pain

we brought with baggage   an inescapable wound

WHITE PERSON
our own grand speculations

RESEARCHER
our desires falling like poisoned stones

ANOTHER CONTINENT
our bodies resting upon others like spiked wood

ALL
absorbing their spirits sex and dignity
in our rapacious endless greed

scene iv

9:35 BLACK BEING NOW
our eyes shaped by legend and myth
seeing in this day what was before

"looking for langston" "paris is burning" "i shall not be moved"
"tongues untied" "brother to brother" "moonlight"

and how now this shapes our troubled hands
we move with that embrace like rolled up sleeves

holding against all things that weigh us down

WHITE PERSON
but this was who he was—

and he had to go and soon
and never let back in

on persian rugs and leather chairs
with urine-sweated jeans wrinkled

odored shirts shit-smelling shoes

his eyes turned sand and milk-white   was he
swaggering in living rooms gazing at groins?

seeking comfort in that heated penetrating hypnotic
lust? that inevitable enviable immediate abandon?

BLACK BEING THEN
but what of his voice? 8 songs for a mad king?
dolmen meredith foss sem feldman sokol

performing stravinky's oedipus rex

and dance—"the moon's silent modulation"
"starr jazzer" and "wood in time" for singleterrry

wanted by boulez—

and his pedicures with kitchen scissors
for homeless men in bowery shelters?

the gifts of his possessions? his
classes with children rolling across the floor?

returning music to trance and play
and standing on stage buffalo pride in 1973?

ANOTHER CONTINENT

the hole in the wall his body's imprint on the door
once site on a staircase shrunken in a corner

falling into recall failing a former lover's hands
before led to the shelter of snow and winds

BLACK BEING NOW

he was asked to be a runaway when he wanted douglas
and his childhood teacher confronted his dreams

as the chair in a canonized sinecure secured
his release while cornell's grand reasoning

found the negative in the affirmative
and a one time lover he thought

wanted him to be a slave

WHITE PERSON

and his brother and mother?
sold their possessions ransacked their space

left little choice for the apartment eviction
the sheriff throwing his scores to the street—

he walked out on rehearsals
came in with whiskey up needled sleeves

then faced front doors he could not open
but was allowed staircases porches front yards—

we were once close then he drove us, and drifted, away

ANOTHER

we met him later in some place we'd rather not name
bare hands over a kettle drum

grinning its flames his bright distant penetrating
elusive eyes as ever daggers targeted our way

BLACK BEING NOW

"coming together" he sang for frederick
followed with melville's attica letters

drowned by the white whale
masked in the state's slaughter

he coveted the black queen in genet
a high scaffold in a long white dress and white mask

revealing his dark face only at the end
following singleterry's grand pas de deux

and black-masked dancers strutting marching
cake-walking tap-dancing the stage—

he held space in brooklyn's community philharmonic
and in the village kitchen

his compositions flowed like whiskey

"if you're so smart, why aren't you rich by now?"
"crazy nigger" "nigger faggot" "sacred songs" "humanity"

"the holy presence of st joan"

he countered attica and stonewall buffalo pride
his class with children and instruments
crawling on floors—

ANCESTOR
and where were you then? when his body sang freedom
and you would not hear?

when he cut the toenails of the homeless
about whom you did not speak?

BLACK BEING THEN
when he cried out for attica
and carried stonewall's wounds?

when he vanished into city streets
after cornell and a record store fell away?

BLACK CHORUS
did you speak to him then? did you
embrace him? and feel his queer blackness

burning his veins?

scene v

14:20 – 16:00 – use quotes from book for audience or dancers – during this time all dancers are in motion with contrasting movements

The issue of race and sexual orientation in late 1960's America, when Julius Eastman was achieving adulthood, were fraught with hostility and humiliation. James Baldwin wrote that to be a Negro in America was to be in a rage almost all the time. The great tennis player Arthur Ashe said in his autobiography that, for him, it was easier to die of AIDS, than to be black in America. "AIDS isn't the heaviest burden I've had to bear," he wrote. Eastman was nearly twenty-nine years old when the Stonewall Inn riots in Greenwich Village protested the perennial police harassment of gays. "To be gay was to risk being continuously called out." As his brother Gerry Eastman remarked, "Julius was black and gay so that was like a double whammy. He had to have double "fuck you" armor to survive." (3)

I lived there with Julius for about a year and a half. We were like brothers. In a way, I liked staying with him because he was always out of town so it was like having the apartment all to myself. Julius paid the rent. I bought the food and helped cook because I knew how, even as a teenager. I knew I was good for Julius because I maintained the house and did the laundry. I was neat. Julius was not. He was slack about housekeeping. I had my own room in another part of the house because, again, Julius would bring people to the house all the time. So I would just go to my room and close the door. To me, it seemed that Burkhardt was the best thing for Julius. Julius was so spaced out and never really took any one person seriously. (27)

scene vi

16:10 RESEARCHER
then there was that gift of magazines
christmas colors burlesque and s & m

beneath sheer paper and thin pink ribbons

the living room with aging grandparents
beside blinking lights and sparkling innocent half-naked angels

tinsel hanging from the window like sperm

and awhile after that tone on the phone
begging a one-time lover to long for memory

that taste of wind and fire in this black spirit
barred by a message to not let him near

what was once home

ANOTHER CONTINENT
and what was it with cage? that man of silence
who admired? heard? chose?

why stage him that way? envy? revenge? tirade
at the complacent academic bourgeoisie?

critique of silence with the noise of a stripped-naked man?

how else was cage to respond? who had opened
his canon to be steeped in a public lust?

there are times docility has its merits
he ignored every one

17:20 BLACK BEING THEN

or did they ignore him? and join the line
of their birth? what we faced when they landed
and in their violent indifference gave us different names?

there was nothing that could be missed
he made himself and was known

the "black queen" in genet
with a white mask revealing himself only at the end

grinning like any other trickster
out before stonewall with attica's blood just behind

banging instruments on the floor with children
finding veins across time in douglas and melville

dragging his lines when he played a runaway slave

BLACK BEING NOW

what blocked him at cornell? purged him
of commissions and performances? and lost him
in such neglect?

it seemed as if the structures he most contested
swallowed his ambition and kicked him away

along with the pangs of that nude performance

colleagues claiming his decadence becoming distant
suspect of an underlying desire he had to move on

scene vii

18:30 GRIOT
how cage was enraged did it lend
to what followed?

that man kneeling stripped naked
and a half-clothed woman running off stage?

an unscripted “song books”
cast without direction or intent

left to instinct and craft—a selection of sudden improvisa-
tions—

but did that morning after cage pounding piano
spike the trail for “hand to mouth”?

less performances and commissions?
the wail of eviction? all notes and scores

books and records thrown to the streets

as cornell’s affirmative action ignored
what his compositions claimed

with a voice more extraordinary than wind
circling in corners a delicate volcanic twist

bound in thin tight sequences an absolute fate
his ambition a separate trait

(to some exasperation)

he would never let anyone near
the cats in the closets, their shit inside

but what of pedicures in shelters? with kitchen scissors?
or the distancing of possessions?

what of foul words children heard
or servicing seekers in subway stalls?

or kissing boots a ritual for sex?

saintly? martyr? majestic? mad?
instead of a sinecure was he the sin to cure?

glitter glitter glitter cheeks and brow
sparkling lashes finger and toe nails

long curly blonde wigs swaying naked necks
rainbow mascara rouge lips and bright teeth

he knew he was treacherous blistering uncertain
his breath contesting guilt in this quagmire of greed

and in the liminal trenches of what some call
"the desert of the real" . . .

scene viii

21:25

FROM *GAY GUERRILLA*

The kids were totally intrigued. Julius started just banging on the floor and the kids banged on the floor, tapping their pencils, tapping on their arms; they were yelling. I suggested they pass out the music so the kids could see the graphic nature of the scores. A lot of these children were taking instrument lessons at school and were used to the standard stuff. Ben and Julius brought the students to the stage so they could see the performance, showing them that the music was not necessarily in a fixed order. That way those kids became collaborators. (35)

The text of Coming Together *is a letter written by Sam Melville, an inmate of Attica prison, who died during the 1971 uprising there. As mentioned earlier, on the morning of September 9, 1971, more than twelve hundred black and Hispanic inmates took control of all five cell blocks at the maximum-security state prison and seized forty-three white guards as hostages. The uprising ended with the deaths of thirty-nine men, both prisoner and hostages, when, four days later, Governor Nelson Rockefeller ordered the State Police to retake the prison by force. An official report issued a year later by the New York State Special Commission on Attica concluded, "With the exception of the Indian Massacres in the late 19th century, the State Police assault which ended the four-day prison uprising was the bloodiest one-day encounter between Americans since the Civil War." (40)*

ACT 4

gay guerrilla

scene: tompkins park

scene i

before the music starts, the black bodies enter one at a time—the last 3 lines in chorus

BLACK BEING THEN
you did not know the reservoir of his queer black rage

nor feel the penetrating vibrations of his heat

you did not taste that sudden splash

self-exile declaration and despair

BLACK BEING NOW
nor smell the stains of this seeming desperation

commissions teaching recordings ending

as if his neck were tied to his heels and his eyes

held to the seemingly impenetrable sorrow of fear

BLACK SPIRIT
to shut down his rebellious discontent

his perilous sex and skin spreading his lips

his calculated critical calling cascading into cage

his penis roaming a world of trembling sex

ANCESTOR
you did not see his anguish in that way

his ass on a quest to sit with the queens of fire

joan margaret katherine micheal the archangel in drag

their tongues martyred in vengeance schooling sharp and
sassy

BLACK CHORUS

his tongue rounding penises between deep white thighs

you did not want the things he saw they would blind you

and turn you into something perilous and free

scene ii

1:00 GRIOT

small town lake erie
unknown population peaking
blacks behind red bank lines

cornell's shadow staining backyards
municipal laced households and white fences
between empty morals hypocritical stop signs
stones and bricks sliced underneath
red-baiting mcarthy curbs of slaughter

always a war—korea cambodia latin
america vietnam—flashing tvs on a nation's screens
two cars in all driveways
dennis the menace leave it to beaver
ozzie/harriet desi/lucy opie/aunt bee
andy/barney/mayberry father knows best
and half-naked cartoon darkies
bones in noses ears and hair
a white man sweating in a cauldron
while amos and andy maintained the myth of skin

a & w root beer bobby soxers tight black pants
patty duke three stooges james dean
marlon brando leather jackets comb in hand
slick cars greased hair
clint eastwood raymond burr
dragnet twilight zone ed sullivan bonanza
licken' chicken shake and bake
a little southern white girl smiling on tv "and i helped!"

banality parading under plush vestments
klan cross burnings a scarlet pederast
churches and sacristies never reveal
their rituals burying sex with sin

so we remember him now as if he were saying
"i could be no less than this
bred in this hybrid sycophancy
of white masks and skin sounds and sex
with the thin limbs and fingers of a black boy
kept in the bubbles of dreams
i dared to burst"

ANCESTOR

it was as if he traveled some white concrete roadway
passing toll booths, cursing cars for days of sorrow
into a nervous falling, light pounding on his eyelids, with
lavender
pillows, the blue heat of hyacinth, their startling birth
pushing thru memory, out of the cold womb.

with scorn and dry, cracked lips
and eloquence, he burned in prayer and mercy, in the sweat-
scented
clothes of the lost and deep forbidden, breaking thru this
tumult, of centuries. in the sirens the streams
of blazing street signs, singed stone
and curbs off broadway and 14th street

BLACK BEING THEN

he took these steps, clear and uneasy, day after day.
into a habititat of emptiness, circle of mud in washington
square park
peddling, like the first time on a bicycle, black
milk thru a twisted white straw, a stranger into envy
out of innocence, then sitting alone on a chess table
in an abandoned park.

and all of this, fragments
that cannot be described, nor could he foretell
what patterned whispers the desperate
might reveal.

scene iii

4:45 non-black chorus as in "evil nigger"

this section follows eastman in some of his homelessness. video captures the crush of night light down barren alleys, with trash containers over-flowing, large black plastic bags strewn about, some open . . . rats . . .

THE RESEARCHER

he walked down narrow   winter streets
those cold sterile places   tompkins park
addicts and potholes   wood rotting
public benches   thick white snow

and each step before him   a tributary
full of laughter and crowded
with sleepless adolescent boys
masturbating in a subway washroom

WHITE PERSON

this told him something sacred   like words
spiraling skyward from a bowl in an open field

frankincense sliding through a halo of thorns
in blue winter air

WHITE PERSON AND RESEARCHER

and with each breeze he continued   his face
caught in the shadows of green gems   ears

loaded into sockets full of pain   cheeks
collapsing into canyons deep as death   and his

forehead brushed like a whisper   formed in the night

eyes weeping as if in a graveyard   at the outskirts
of dark and noisy tents   of a tropical bazaar

ANCESTOR

with this dry wind
a current, in high trees the spastic air

the blue circumference
all things are measured by, benchmarks
undiscovered, sitting
in his heart

the color of hibiscus, yellow and red
stems stretched into passion, whatever it was
he believed held more than he asked for

a curved alabaster
shell, hollowed
polished,
a finished gem

BLACK BEING NOW

this was the distance he lived with
so he walked, sometimes
into night, when the moon shone
on pale streets—
the flushed face
of a poker player—and the cool air
whined like a saxophone
over his indifference

if you listened, his voice
was everywhere, in the edge
of the sirens, church
bells and cabbies' lips, caught
in the pattern of driving rain
where you could hear him

even if you closed your ears
and his mouth fell silent
with whispers floating   like vapor
down evening hills . . .

BLACK BEING THEN

other times he woke slowly
and lay on his bed   a stranger in a shelter

awaiting doors to open   beyond
the fading   feuding distance of sleep

where silence was a blur   on chipped walls
of memory   and he could feel

the forced pressures   of an hypnotic stare
with eyes   outside bedsheets

and twilight   hovering above waters
an eastern screen   set a tired sun

into its calm blue depths
its casual ignorance

as each day became an adventure
of skies opening to him saints in chorus

singing fortunes   for the bereaved
with trumpets blossoming sorrow

horns faded into shadows   their
sharp heights   stabbing the bewildered dark

like fireflies glimmering night lights
on a small boat caught
in a turbulent sea

WHITE PERSON

despite this
somehow he seemed to be
the one who understood little

about sweat and alcohol
opium needles a heroin fix
the daily deliberate haze
the passing winter and spring
put out by night's hesitant hand

like a sacrifice lounging in resistance
he went into cold trembling
silent spaces wounds in the heart
evidence of all mysteries

BLACK BEING NOW

you, however, will remember from earlier
years: his assured voice, dark eyes, lean
cheeks, his do-rag and dreads, balance
between bitterness and hope, anger
and fearlessness, his voice singing down, how
the powerful play, and pray, his optimism
and the weight under his finger tips, lean
thighs and calves, slight waist, now gone
absorbed into that delirium spirit leaves

RESEARCHER

perhaps it was in this distance
when he sat in a café
with langston ellison baldwin
nietzsche coltrane monk?
and a bell rang like a pacemaker
inside his heart, the doorway
full of rain, full of the dampened
tongues of prophecy, opening
out to the arms of a child

whose innocence
unmasks treachery, history?
his thin fingers, grasping the edges
of a rare storm, the doorknob to
this theatre of senseless doom?

ANCESTOR

and in these unknown journeys, did he dream of the homeless
who were everywhere, streets of new york buffalo ithaca?
did he recognize the one true christian conviction?
the poor will always be with us, and there will always be
those keeping it that way, while everything else,
we now know, must be personal like the one
outside he let in who took what little
he had gathered through his endless dreams

scene iv

9:50 – 12:10

while audience reads, dancers can come out of their pattern for duets, trios, ensemble, etc. weave in dancers words from crp

FROM *GAY GUERRILLA*

> *Ithaca did not have a large black population in the 1950's and 1960's. When asked, neither Professor Sokol, nor Julius's high school classmates, could pinpoint incidents of racism. In fact, one of Julius's classmates wrote, "We were in a science club project, and even then one could see he was extra smart and a very talented young man. There was . . . no race cards to be played in those days. . . . Ithaca was a good place to grow up in."*
>
> *Frances Eastman saw it somewhat differently, however. Julius had been singing since grade school, and was an admired soloist in the high school glee club, even winning an award from the Hollis Dann Glee Club Fund, which had been established in 1945 to be given to an outstanding glee club member. She thought his grades were good, but near the end of his senior year, the school counselor called her in for discussion of college possibilities, and said "no school will accept Julius." To Mrs. Eastman, it just didn't add up. She knew that the counselor had taken pains with two young girls in Julius's class who wanted to go to Bryn Mawr, making sure they were invited to the proper teas and such. Yet for Julius, the counselor couldn't think of anything to promote his candidacy for admission to a college. (13)*
>
> *In mid-February of the 1974-75 academic year, Eastman received a letter from the Office of the Provost, informing him that he was not being recommended for a renewal of his appointment. "I am obliged to inform you officially that the*

[following] 1975-76 academic year will be your terminal year." Several factors are mentioned in his file, among them a 1974 memo from the acting chairman of the Music Department regarding unannounced absences from classes, lack of notification from him stating that he would be on tour, or what arrangements he had made to cover his classes while he was away. (42)

Although he had the option of remaining at the university for an additional year, Eastman wrote to James Blackhurst, the acting Music Department chairman, on April 7: "Dear Mr. Blackhurst: In order to further my professional career, I will resign from SUNY as of September 1975." On April 14, Blackhurst replied: "I have received your resignation letter. . . . There are many here who will miss you."

Files on the music faculty committee meetings, if they still exist, are not available, hence it is impossible to know any details of the discussion or the vote count. (43)

scene v

12:20 BLACK BEING THEN
and in this distant distinct district of disputes
did he see in departures those he knew

exhaling memories from far away
after that naked angel pierced him

with that sharp and dirty dart of indignation
from cage on stage glittering anger

pounding the piano across borders
a sudden blending of canon and composition

glowing under a privileged shade
that strayed from such love of silence?

to push this sexed-raced-radical trangressor
from studios stages classrooms?

to spaces where his body's tendrils could only land him
between the ill-tempered fusion of flames and air?

BLACK BEING NOW
did he indulge these thoughts in flashes of fatigue?

hunger for love in moments when
all energy seemed lost in a piano quartet?

beaming a structure of notes compelled
against a sky of classical obedience

he set mastered usurped

then followed down aisles
back alleys cellars of anxieties

like one who had visited the dead
seeking to share the treasures of this sleep

BLACK BEING THEN AND NOW

after years wandering rooms of the unknown
he leapt thru narrow hallways

away from chalkboards
and powder white markings of intellect

away from classrooms wild with words
he read to recant as if exposed

away from the blurred twisted edges of hate
into a sacristy of solitude and sudden leavings

RESEARCHER

did he then pick grief stones   out of the flowing
river cool as death   cool as the moment when all air
fell into summer   a solemn hollow memory?

it was as if a swift current   met and absorbed him
as he watched and waited   motionless as an effigy
shaped by barbed wire   and covered with tar—

WHITE PERSON

cloud into mist   wings spread over the dull brown earth
did he look into the pensive night   for a deliberate fortune
locked in the crumbling skies   temples of wondering?
carved into white marble   during an early frost in fields
first days of october   with the light of ice-tinged
dew   jabbing the damp electric air?

ANOTHER CONTINENT

did he stride thru contemplation   into a crematorium
of anxiety   a fall moon balanced on the cut edge of dawn
in a time when he was blessed   with deliverance?

the stigmata of smooth white stones   weeping openly
between tight fingers and clenched fists—   did they drip thru
become rooted in the earth   seedlings of sorrow?   disorder?

NON-BLACK CHORUS
did he become the litigant of pain?
its words   passed through sleeplessness

his eyes rolled into a wisdom   where he saw nothing
but heard the cries of night   inside a theatre

where hope sat   a silenced symphony—

RESEARCHER
was this his crossing   point of memory?
gliding like a quiet   questionable angel in shadow

without the mercies of slaughter   the slow
and fevered nuptials   of fear?

WHITE PERSON
was this his limbo?   mirrors frozen into smoke
over his remains   his thin body of glancing night

crushed against sharp edges   of composition
music sheets spread like thorns   across a table of disbelief?

ANOTHER CONTINENT
was this the finale   of his vanishings?
his colleagues hedged against him   amidst the calculus
of cage and chance   his raw bloodied moment of despair

angle of torment   walking away from everything
as if an exile   in the beet red forests veiled in truth?

NON-BLACK CHORUS

where he felt a blunt shaft   wandering always in riot
between violent abstract   pages of night
as he sat   defiantly alone

ANCESTOR

and in that descending evening of madness, when he stood,
at the precipice
wind whipping him, a torrent of suffering, wild and unyielding.
black scarf fluttering, black-peaked cap, black lapel. an
essence
of his deliberate ease, those mostly pyrrhic moments when
his heart and veins, their shallow perforated vessels
disturbing slowness, plunged downward into a drain. out of
hell
and its lesser places, the ever present challenging
passages of silence, prayer and grace, did he come to
reveal, the studious pistons of his birth

BLACK BEING THEN

as they hammered him, again and again, out of ignorance
into the wet winter wind, boomerang blistering cold, it was
as if i saw him, then, a forager in a courtyard, a lonely warrior
clinging like ice, to a piece of bent copper
on a skyscraper's ledge, he looked at this as if he
were carrying music sheets in a picnic basket
full of dried white and red roses, in bloom.

scene vi

17:50 – 20:10 audience reading

all dancers in and out as with other audience reading

FROM *GAY GUERRILLA*

Hill recalls that, although everybody liked Julius Eastman, trying to get along with him day after day was hard. Eastman had voluntarily left his job with the Brooklyn Philharmonia's community concert series and, although seemingly in good shape, was having trouble getting to work. "He wasn't getting work because he was a son of a bitch," says Hill. "He would lay down obstacles, make things difficult for people. Somehow, he felt that it was his mission. You could say that he martyred himself. It didn't seem like a racial issue, since he did it so deliberately. To this day, I have never met anyone who was more an architect of his own fate." (58)

Hill Continues:

For the first two months we lived together Julius insisted on calling me Ananda. He'd use tidbits from Buddhist discipline or little proverbs about Allah—and the "thank you Jesus" thing—a little too loud, like an attention-getting ploy. What he was saying was "I'm not just an artist; I'm beyond that."

And he lived the titles of his music. He was the crazy nigger and the gay guerilla. He was fearsome. He played out those roles. He was an uncompromising man. He liked the idea that he was a "nigger." He loved that because it put him in the position of transgressing some sort of bourgeois status. He liked the idea that he was gay and he pushed it to the extreme. He was filthy dirty. He was a slob. That was the role he wanted to play. He took aspects of his identity and foisted them on people in this provocative way.

So he's living in the apartment I gave him. The next thing I know is that he's gotten evicted. He's not making any money. He didn't pay his rent. They [the city marshal] took all his music, his art, and everything else out of the apartment. Julius is saying that he needs a place to stay. I say "Julius, what do you mean, you need a place to stay? Where is all your shit?" "Oh," he says, "the sheriff came and took it." "Where is it?" I say. "Oh, I don't want that shit anymore," he says. (56)

He was letting it go. My wife felt uneasy when he came by because he was acting crazy. He lost his address book in The Toilet. He couldn't be bothered to pay his rent. He made no effort to reclaim his belongings, which I found out later had been confiscated to a warehouse in Brooklyn. "Julius," I said, "How could you let this happen?" He answered, "It was an inconsistent period." (56)

scene vii

20:35 GRIOT
cool air danced in the light
like a thought in the brain   fluid

with speed   a temporary settling—

thru a crack in a cloud   an eye
inside my skull   he appeared

suddenly in the summer sky   like a hang glider
riding between   childhood and memory

his face travelling a meridian
where even pathfinders   get lost—

the fading colors of an august evening
a spread of azalea shimmering on water

i sat beside a dock   at the fulton street market
thinking of him   the streets he once wandered

corners kept   dark walkways of regret
cold pavements   now gentrified

even tho he slept there   some times
in the company of others   a darling

of the elements   visiting shelters and old beds
and a home with nothing other   than sky as roof—

a thin balding man   at night stoking the coke fumes
of an industrial drum   did he watch wild sparks

flirt about his shirt   like june bugs?
and see the fading orange brush strokes

of evening   dying behind buildings
in a city he once called home?

the boy who sang down choirs
and grinned over piano keys   did he realize

death was not in the distance   but matched him
stride for stride   like a beast snarling in the hedgerows

of a public park?

WHITE PERSON

did a world of asphalt become him?
dandelions in the cracks   their heads
pushing up   against the shafts of night?

did he imagine chain-link fences   around him
high as his waist   a continent containing him
as if he were a creature   carrying an enormous

shell of porcelain and jade?

wild morning glories   old grey houses
and the bugles of saints—   did they sound him
as if to acknowledge   there were sentries

to the borders   he roamed?

ANOTHER CONTINENT

other times   i thought i saw him in bright mornings
crawling down alleys of torment   like a child
on a journey   singing in a chorus about heaven—

what i heard was no secret   the faint
rustling of cats   squeals of cornered rats
while the sky bent downward   like a butler

reserving a brown patch of earth   he felt he earned
as if he were a paper boy   collecting an amount overdue

RESEARCHER

in another time or place   far from this inertia
he might have forsaken this calling   this life

as an innocent who heard   the trumpet notes
of an easter lily   scale the years of suffering

until death appeared at his bedside   a dry cleaner
carrying a black suit   and a bill

BLACK BEING THEN

sometimes i thought he might   have gone into anything
especially an eternity   bright as a raincoat—

but winters however were a bitch   it was
almost as if he felt he needed   to have sex
with each cold spell   as if a prolonged
fuck   would bring him warmth—

so did he pray each night   for a virgin full of fire
an incendiary temptation?   strolling by a trash heap
outside tompkins park   waiting for church bells

to sound out a new day   hoping that
out of the marginal   spirit of spheres a man
would be born   to fill his hunger with longing?

the purity of virtue?   a night in front of a glowing fireplace
far from the back alleys   of death?

ANCESTOR

or did he envision a voyage   and looking out
the back window   of a bus or speeding car?

behind him   a monolith of buildings fading
in a polluted haze   stretches of forests and farmlands

BLACK BEING NOW

endless fields   cows horses sheep
cask of whiskey   pouch of crystal dust

backdrop to dirt roads   old barns standing like straw
and a rambling barking dog   carrying a water bottle and a map

to lead him to a treasure   at the end of a one-way ticket home

ANOTHER CONTINENT AND RESEARCHER

it seemed nothing could deter him
he was convinced   he must go on a journey

manhatten to buffalo   only to confirm
that this city   will grant him a black box

and a spot under a plot of dirt—

WHITE PERSON

and when there   he would find his way through
the thin lights of highways   to where it all started

and ended with very few knowing   until eight months after
a shock of words in the village voice

proclaimed he had finally   moved on

scene viii

AUDIENCE AND DANCERS

FROM *GAY GUERRILLA*

In May 1989, Julius Eastman returned to Buffalo.

He came to my house and my friend Haj went to the door but wouldn't let him in. Haj didn't know Julius but, from my description, he must have realized who it was. Haj telephoned me at the hospital where I was working and his description of Julius was awful. It seems that Julius had slept on the grass in front of my house or in the neighbor's across the street. I told Haj not to let him in. (63)

Even before Julius left Buffalo back in the summer of 1976, I was beginning to withdraw from him because I was a little nervous and scared of him. I wouldn't let him come up to my apartment anymore. I got that type of fear about him. He was so strange, you know. He had this "open life" and everybody should just put up with it.

Then one late Saturday afternoon fourteen years later, there he was on Main and High Street in Buffalo. He was puny and not very healthy looking. I realized he must have been facing financial problems. I didn't have a lot of money either, but I know I gave him some—how much I can't recall. He said he was staying in a shelter around Main near Riley Street. I think it was operated by some Catholic nuns. It was about 6:00 P.M., so we talked and we said goodbye there on Main Street.

Within a week I got a call from the hospital saying that he was dead. He had given my telephone number to the staff there. From what I understand, he had been in the hospital for a couple of days. I felt real bad that I sort of forced him aside, but I just knew that I couldn't take Julius to my home and deal with him and his way of life anymore. So I separated from him right on that corner. (64)

What do we know about Julius Eastman? We know he was gifted, ambitious, magnetic, theatrical, with an elegant bearing, a beautiful smile, and a beautiful voice; we know he was impatient and stubborn, arrogant (sometimes), also modest; he was intelligent, undisciplined, highly sexual, dismissive about money and "things." He was also a spiritual man; a searcher who could be a fearsome boundary-crosser, a trickster. We know he was a man of two worlds, probably at home in neither. Ultimately, Julius Eastman could not resolve his contradictions. As he veered more and more into turmoil, he lost his footing in the real world and could no longer do the work to honor his gift. (63)

NEXT GENERATION AND BLACK BEING NOW

- i did not know he had such a profound influence on north america's music creation. i did not know he died alone. i did not know he fought a battle against racism and homophobia in his work, art and life. like a river he was simply looking for the sea. i did not know any of that.
- i didn't know he had trinidadian lineage. i didn't know his music. i didn't know how such genius and bravery could have existed within such a vessel of a body. i didn't know him.
- his images are very archetypal, leading us to believe he was deeply connected to another world. he was a creative fire. a very spiritual person yet with a disturbed mind. he looks like he is pure. a dreamer.
- he was a musical genius. he was american. he was black. he was queer. he possessed a mystical creative gift. a mind that could not rest ever. he was at the avant garde of new music creation, but never really fully recognized.

excerpts on pages 29-30, 46, 51, 65-66, 71-72, and 77-78 are from *Gay Guerrilla: Julius Eastman and His Music,* edited by Renee Levine Packer and Mary Jane Leach (Rochester, NY: U of Rochester Press, 2018).

in researching this work, it was important to explore precolonial sexual activities in Africa before the impact of colonization. i went in this direction since i was certain that the values and restrictions of heteronormativity were imposed by colonial powers whose accounts set out to describe same sex intimacies as being deviant and in conflict with their christian beliefs.

the sources i was able to explore were:

Books

1. Murray, Stephen O and Will Roscoe, eds. *Boy Wives and Female Husbands: Studies in African Homosexualities*. Palgrave, 1998
2. Amadiume, Ifi. *Male Daughters, Female Husbands: Gender and Sex in African Society. London*: Zed Books, 1987, 2015.
3. Epprecht, Marc. *Heterosexual Africa: The History of an Idea From the Age of Exploration to the Age of Aids*. Athens, Ohio: Ohio UP. and Durban: U of Kwazulu-Natal Press, 2008
4. Hoad, Neville. *African Intimacies: Race, Homosexuality and Globalization*. Minneapolis: U of Minnesota Press, 2007
5. Tinsley, Omise'eke Natasha. *Black Atlantic, Queer Atlantic: Queer Imaginings of the Middle Passage*. Durham, NC: Duke UP, 2008.

Articles

1. Bertolt, Boris. "The Invention of Homophobia in Africa." http://creativecommons.org/licences/by/4.0)
2. Epprecht, Marc. "'Bisexuality'" and the Politics of Normal in African Ethnography." *Anthropologica* 48 (2008): 187-201.
3. Epprecht, Marc. "The Making of "African Sexuality: Early Sources, Current Debates." in *Sexual Diversity in Africa*. (2013): 54-66.

4. Evaristo, Bernardine. "The idea that homosexuality was a colonial import is a myth." *The Guardian*, March 8, 2014.
5. "Expanded Criminalisation of Homosexuality in Uganda." Sexual Minorities Uganda (SMUG), January 2004
6. Makofane, Keletso. "Unspoken facts: a history of homosexualities in Africa." *Culture, Health & Sexuality*. 15 (2013) S114-S116.
7. McKaiser, Eusebius. "Homosexuality un-African? The claim is an historical embarrassment." *The Guardian*, Oct. 2, 2012.
8. Msibi, T. "The Lies We Have Been Told: On (Homo) Sexuality in Africa." *Africa Today*. 58,1 (2011): 55-77.
9. Ochieng, Sidney. "Homosexuality in Pre-colonial Kenya." https:// sydney ochieng.co.ke/category/activism.
10. OckyDub. "Homosexuality in Sub-Saharan Africa." https:cypheravenue.com/author/ocky.
11. Schmidt, Heike I. "Colonial Intimacy: The Rechenberg Scandal and Homosexuality in German East Africa." *Journal of the History of Sexuality*. 17,1 (2008): 25-59.
12. Stewart, Colin. "21 Varieties of traditional African homosexuality." 76crimes.com/2014/01/30.
13. Tamale, S. "Confronting the Politics of Nonconforming Sexualities in Africa." *African Studies Review*. 56, 2(2013): 31-45.
14. Yoruba, Cosmic. "Homosexuality and African history: the roots of the criminalisation of homosexuality." https://76crimes.com/2014/01/30/21-varieties-of-traditional-african-homosexuality/

TERMS USED IN THE POEMS

Azanda/Zande – Boy Wives p. 26/27, African Intimacies p. 56, The idea that homosexuality was a colonial import is a myth, p.2, Expanded Criminalisation of Homosexuality in Uganda, A Flawed Narrative p. 9,

Bala Bitesha – Boy Wives p. 146

Chagkacha – Boy Wives p. 33

Eshenga – Boy Wives p. 147

Fon Boys – Boy Wives p. 280

Gaglo – Boy Wives p. 105 and 280

Ganga-Ya-Chibanda – Boy Wives p. 10, Expanded Criminalisation of Homosexuality in Uganda, A Flawed Narrative p. 9, Varieties of traditional African homosexuality, p.2

Gor-Digen – Boy Wives p. 107 and 282

Hanithi – Boy Wives p. 30

Khanith – Boy Wives p. 74 and 77

Lagerdis – Boy Wives p. 102/103

Londos – Boy Wives p. 280

Malungo – Black Atlantic p. 198

Malungue Batiment – Black Atlantic p. 198

Mashoga – Boy Wives p. 31-33, 76-87

Mati – Black Atlantic p. 198

Mbenda – Boy Wives p. 71

Mirundi Priests – Boy Wives p.282

Mudoka Dako Awes – Boy Wives p. 35, Varieties of traditional African homosexuality, p.2 (cited as Mukodo Dako), Expanded Criminalisation of Homosexuality in Uganda, A Flawed Narrative p. 9,

ACKNOWLEDGEMENTS

1. I've received grants from the Toronto Arts Council, Ontario Arts Council and Canada Council for the Arts for the research on and writing of these poems.

2. Some of these poems have appeared in *The Changing Face of Canadian Literature* edited by Dane Swan, Guernica Press.

3. I want to express my deepest appreciation for the members of the 'wind in the leaves collective' who have inspired me and worked through many rehearsals that contributed to the editing and refinement of these poems. These folks are: Kevin A. Ormsby, Rodney Diverlus, Laurence Lemieux, You Ugai, Bakari Lindsay, Shannon Litzenberger, Michael Mortley, Ana Claudette Groppler, Kelly Juenesse, Morgyn Aronyk-Schell, Mateo Galindo Torres, Aria Evans, Claire Whitaker, Mayumi Lashbrook, Deltin Sejour.

4. I also want to thank the editors/authors of *Gay Guerrilla*, the book about Julius Eastman. Both Renee Levine Packer and Mary Jane Leach were quite generous with their time speaking with me about Julius Eastman.

5. And, as always, a special thanks to my wife, Bia Rohde, without whom none of this could be done.